DOT-TO-DOT COUNT TO 50 FOR BOYS + COLORING WORKBOOK

FUN CONNECT THE DOTS FOR AGES 5 AND UP

FUNKEY BOOKS

CONTENTS

You can find more of our books
on Amazon!

Simply search for "Funkey Books"
on www.amazon.com.

Hi there _____!
(Your Name)

Thank you so much for connecting dots with us.
Get ready because this is going to be fun!

This is how it works... Take your pencil and
connect the dots from number 1 to 50.
After you're done, you can finish your beautiful
picture by coloring it in!

*HINT: The puzzles start out a bit easier and
then get more challenging as the number count
increases.

Have fun and happy connecting!
Enjoy coloring in your beautiful works of art.

LET'S GET STARTED

1-10

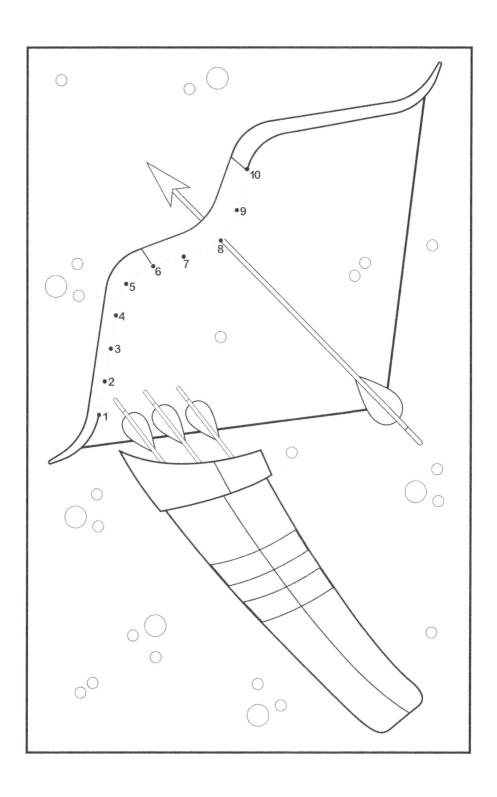

CHARACTERS
& PROFESSIONS
1-20

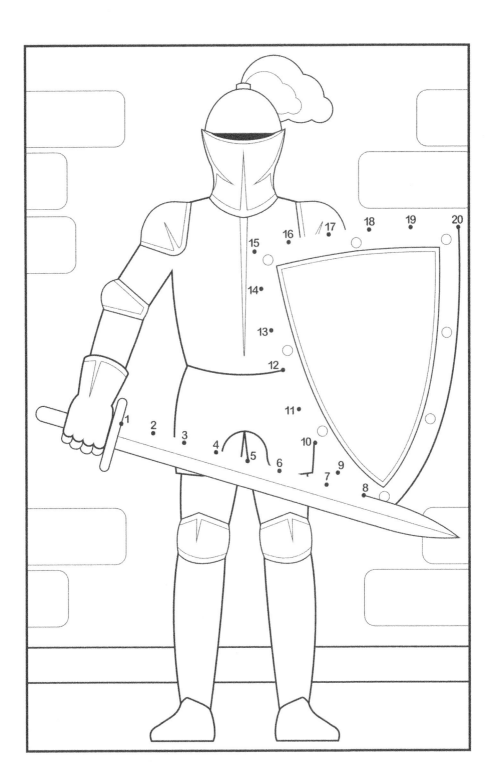

ANIMALS & MYTHICAL CREATURES

1-30

SPORTS & ACTIVITIES

1-40

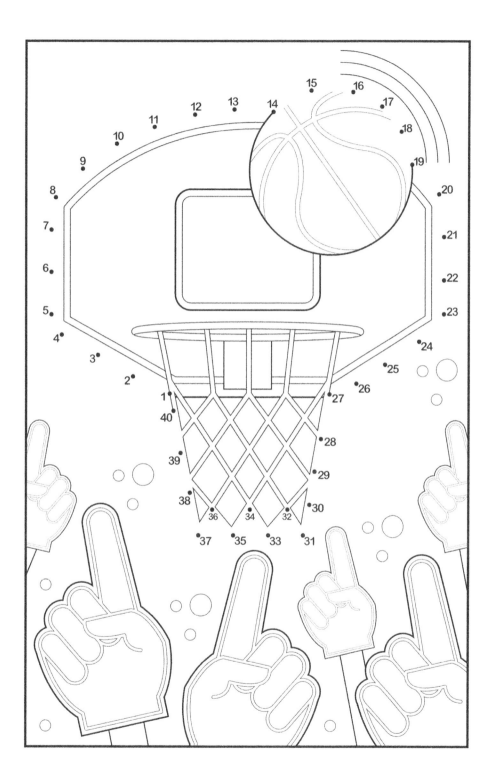

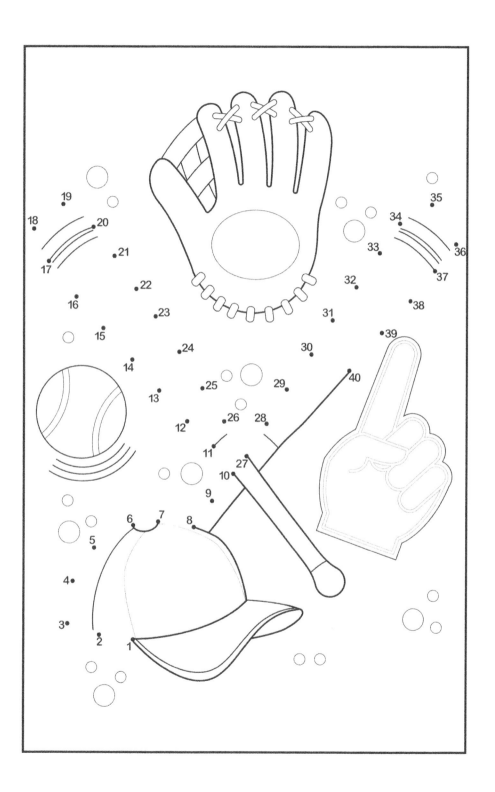

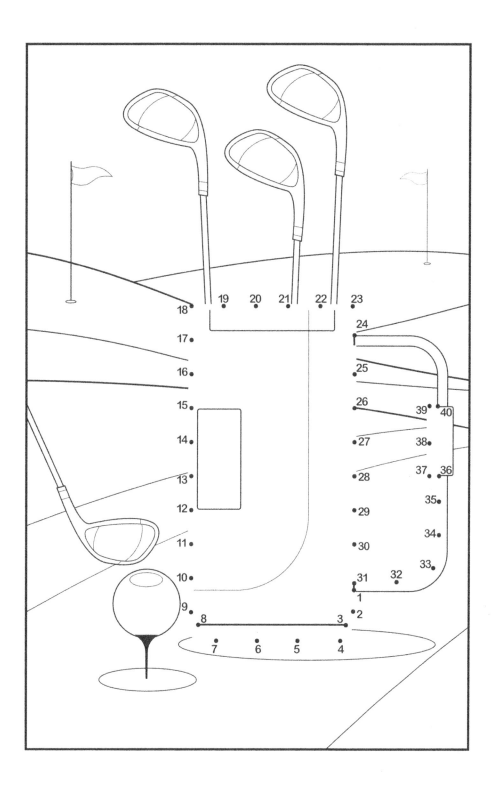

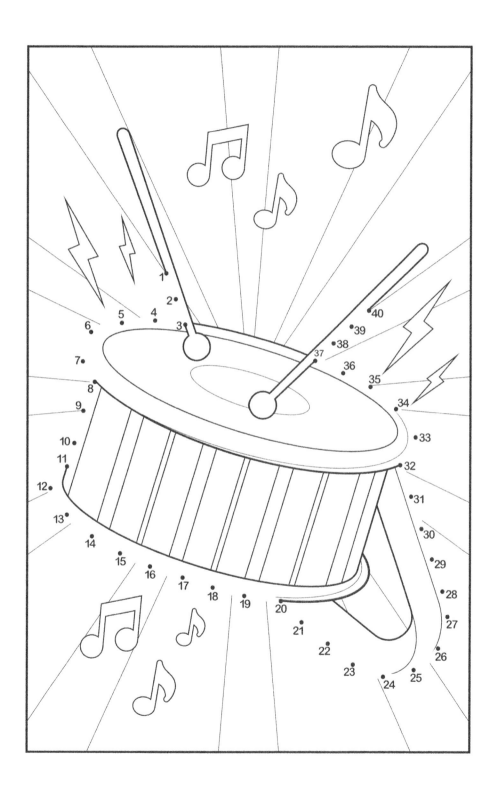

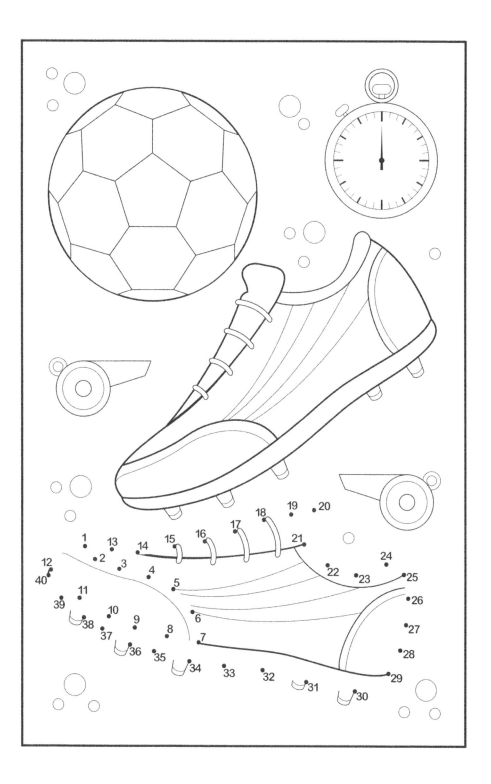

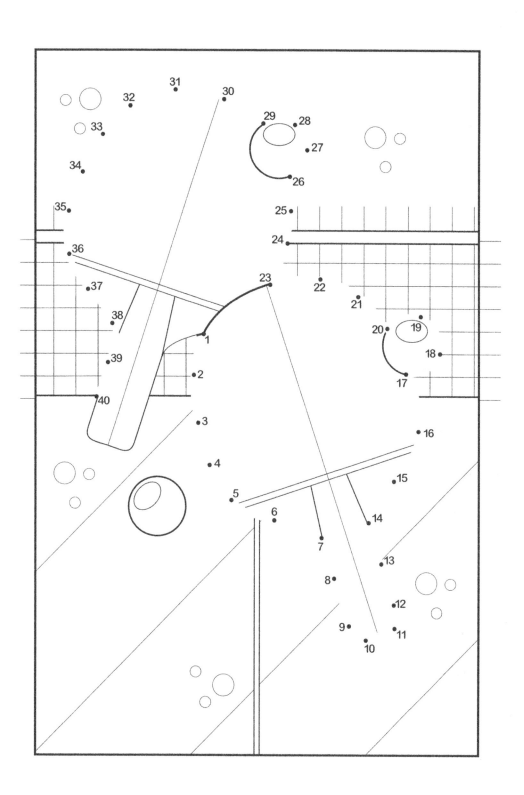

A DAY AT THE FIRE STATION

1-50

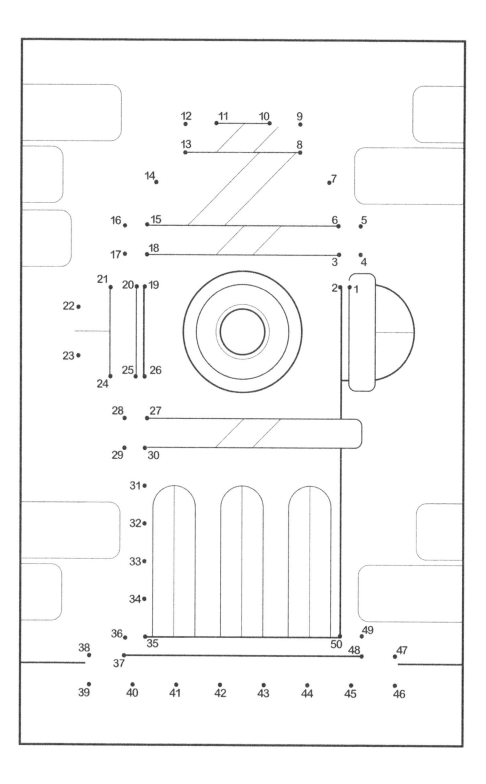

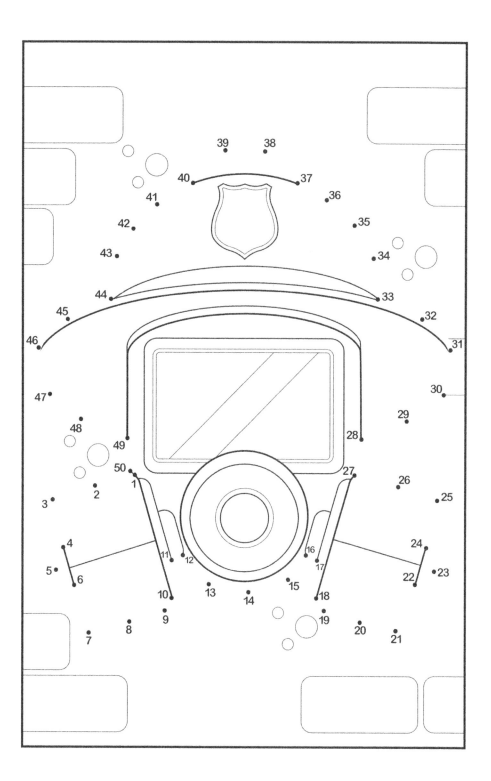

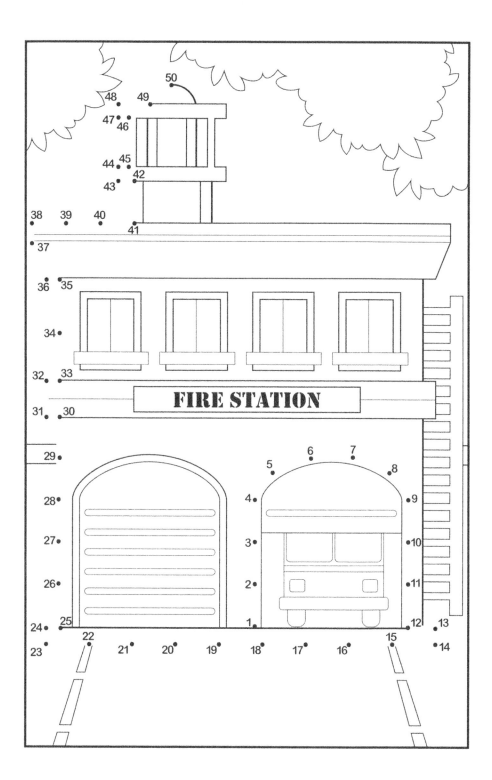

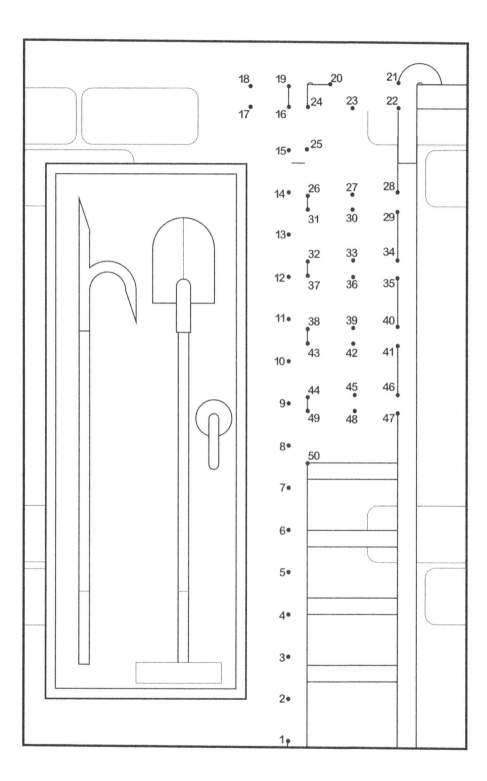

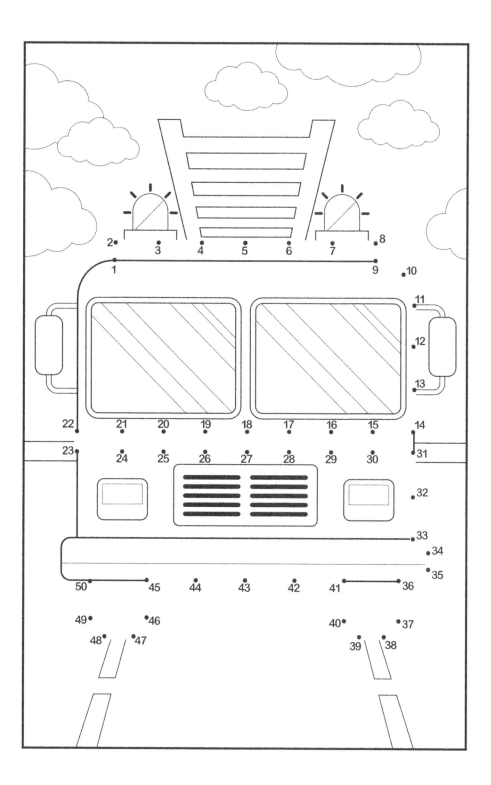

WOW! Great Work!

You did it! You connected all of the dots
and colored in all of the pages.

Very impressive stuff!

If you enjoyed completing these dot-to-dot
puzzles, we would love to hear about it.
You can do this by leaving a review wherever
you purchased this book. We love getting
feedback from our puzzlers and connectors.

Thank you very much and have an
awesome day!

Made in the USA
Monee, IL
02 November 2020